The Little Book
Boxes for R

Ideas for collections of items to support role play in the Foundation Stage

Written by Ann Roberts
Illustrations by Liz Persse
Series Editor - Sally Featherstone

The Little Book of Prop Boxes for Role Play

ISBN 1 902233 63 8

©Featherstone Education Ltd, 2001
Text ©Ann Roberts, 2001
Published October 2001
Reprinted January 2002
Reprinted November 2002

'Little Books' is a trade mark of Featherstone Education Ltd

Little Books ™

Published in the United Kingdom by
Featherstone Education Ltd
44 - 46 High Street
Husbands Bosworth
Leicestershire
LE17 6LP

Prop Boxes for Role Play

What are prop boxes?

Prop boxes contain objects/resources that form a collection linked to a specific role play focus or a series of linked activities. Practitioners invest valuable time in gathering resources as they prepare a role play situation, and when the focus changes, these resources often seem to dissolve and disappear. When you need the resources 12 months later, you spend time again collecting them. Prop boxes enable you to organise role play and easily revisit those ideas which children particularly enjoy or which are recurring themes in your setting.

The concept of the Prop Box is to facilitate storage and easy retrieval, and boxes with lids enable easy stacking. Many settings are short of storage space, so prop boxes enable you to organise the spaces you have.

Containers

Using a set of identical containers makes life easier.

Here are some ideas:

- ❖ plastic boxes
- ❖ stacking crates with or without lids
- ❖ strong cloth bags with draw strings
- ❖ sturdy cardboard boxes, covered in wallpaper or plastic
- ❖ vegetable racks

Each box should be clearly labelled and should contain a list of contents.

Contents of the boxes

Focusing on a theme or scenario for a prop box does not mean that activities are restricted. In fact the contents of the boxes allow for a range of play - children will often use the resources in a totally different way from that intended by adults. The prop boxes explored in this book contain a basic set of resources, you will certainly find more things to add, and more themes to explore.

Prop boxes are not just a receptacle for resources, they are sophisticated tools for practitioners. In each box, you should consider including labels, books, posters, writing and maths resources, music, songs and rhymes, tapes, videos etc. In each box there will be sufficient resources for different aspects of the theme. For example the 'Rock a Bye Baby' box equipment will suit a baby ward in a hospital, bringing a baby home and a baby clinic. You should also consider whether you need more than one of some items to allow for flexible, simultaneous play in different parts of your setting by different groups of children.

Managing the boxes

Prop boxes need setting up, they also need managing and updating. You will want to evaluate and add new equipment to existing boxes. You will want to make new collections. The items in the box should be as high **quality** as you can find and afford. Some of course will be 'consumable' and will need replacing, all will need cleaning and checking for **damage and replacement**. Labels need **monitoring** for accurate spelling and quality of print. **Other languages** and artefacts should be reflected in your boxes wherever possible, even if you work in a monocultural setting. Clothes and artefacts should reflect both **genders** and a range of **cultures**. Children with **special needs** should have right of access to all activities.

Each box will introduce new **vocabulary**. Word banks should also be included and added to as the boxes are used, providing useful words for all adults working in the setting.

All staff should be involved in these activities, and **parents and children** can make useful suggestions and contributions to the contents of boxes. Ongoing notes and new suggestions should also be included; this will broaden the scope and contents of the boxes, and ideas for their possible use. (You may wish to use the **photo-copiable letter to parents** and the evaluation sheet included at the end of this book.)

Children should be involved in the selection for and care of equipment in the boxes, checking it and putting it away after use. Children could also be invited to suggest ideas for new boxes and their contents.

4

How do prop Boxes help to promote high quality play?

It is now widely recognised that children need many different kinds of role play, and two or more simultaneous areas stimulate a higher level of play. For example, a pizza place and a domestic area, or a post office inside and a parcel office outside will stimulate interaction between two groups of children.

Changes in our environment are important to us all. Have you noticed an area in your setting which is under used by the children? Are you concerned that the children do not understand the purposes of the resources in the role play area, or are using them inappropriately? Do you think the children have become bored with the range of items or the focus of this area?

These are all indicators of a need for a change, and one way to start is to introduce just one or two of the props from a new box to create interest among the children. Of course you could mix and match the contents of more than one box, returning the things to the correct box at the end of the session or when interest wanes.

Prop boxes encourage children to experiment, approaching the world of role play with enthusiasm and imagination.

For each of the boxes in this book you will find:

- ❖ a list of objects and resources for the box (you will find more)
- ❖ ideas for larger resources, furniture and equipment useful to the theme of the box
- ❖ some suggested activities linked to the focus (for small and larger groups)
- ❖ some stories, songs and rhymes (add copies of these to boxes)
- ❖ relevant Early Learning Goals for the activities and experiences

At the end of the book you will find:

- ❖ a photocopiable contents and monitoring sheet
- ❖ a photocopiable letter to parents encouraging them to send things for the boxes
- ❖ a full list of the titles and publishers of the stories we include.

Links with the Early Learning Goals for the Foundation Stage

The prop boxes in this Little Book support the stepping stones and the objectives in the Early Learning Goals. If your prop boxes link to your planning you will have a good resource base, which is ready to use as you approach each theme or children become interested in an activity.

Early Learning Goals linked to role play are:

Personal and social development
- Work as part of a group or class, taking turns and sharing fairly, understanding that there need to be agreed values, and codes of behaviour for groups of people, including adults and children, to work together harmoniously;
- Select and use activities and resources independently

Language, communication and literacy
- Use language to imagine and recreate roles and experiences
- Interact with others, negotiating plans and activities and taking turns in conversations;
- Attempt writing for various purposes, using features of different forms such as lists, stories, instructions

Knowledge and Understanding of the World
- Find out about, and identify some features of living things, objects and events they observe;
- Ask questions about why things happen and how things work;
- Build and construct with a wide range of objects, selecting appropriate resources, and adapting their work where necessary;
- Observe, find out and identify features in the place they live and the natural world

Physical Development
- Move with confidence, imagination and in safety;
- Move with control and co-ordination;
- Use a range of small and large equipment

Creative Development
- Move with confidence, imagination and in safety;
- Use their imagination in music, dance, imaginative and role play and stories

Contents

Title and focus of prop box
'Twitchers Paradise - The Bird Hide'
Focus - watching birds and other wildlife

Contents of prop box

- ❖ binoculars - made or bought
- ❖ bird recognition chart (RSPB)
- ❖ camera - made or real
- ❖ recording of bird song
- ❖ reference books of birds, eggs and nests
- ❖ camouflage net with leaves and twigs on
- ❖ artificial or plastic bird models
- ❖ large box, screen or house corner frame
- ❖ clipboards, pens, pencils
- ❖ plain paper for observations
- ❖ bird pictures, labelled with bird parts
- ❖ casual clothes for bird watchers (shorts, hats, tee shirts
- ❖ laminated photos of garden birds for spotting
- ❖ plan of the garden
- ❖ photocopies of bird drawings
- ❖ whiteboard for spotting chart
- ❖ stickers with bird pictures for recording
- ❖ feathers and empty nests (spray first!)
- ❖ plan of the garden
- ❖ bird feeders
- ❖ bird food (only feed birds in the winter!)
- ❖ pictures of bird footprints

Suggested activities

- ❖ site the bird hide inside, by a window to observe real birds. Make a daily record.
- ❖ site the bird hide outside in summer.
- ❖ play bird song recordings in the background to create an atmosphere.
- ❖ make bird cake in winter, and record who comes (recipe in back of book).
- ❖ make an exhibition with pretend birds in plastic cases. Add mounted children's pictures of birds and their bird spotting charts and photos.
- ❖ make collages with feathers and shells.

Rhymes & stories

- ❖ Four and Twenty Black Birds
- ❖ Two Little Dickey Birds
- ❖ The Birdy Song
- ❖ Lance's Lunchtime*
- ❖ The Lighthouse Keeper's Lunch*
- ❖ Hello Beaky?

Curriculum links

- ❖ PSD: caring for birds: working in pairs & groups
- ❖ LCL: vocabulary (parts & names of birds)
- ❖ M: counting/ordering numbers
- ❖ K/u: living things; observation
- ❖ Phys: flight, speed
- ❖ Cr: explore colour, texture, shape and form

Title and focus of prop box
'Let's Celebrate Diwali'
Focus - an example of a festival box. Try others.

Contents of prop box

❖ Diwali cards
❖ clay divas
❖ candles
❖ writing materials
❖ bags, purses, money
❖ posters and photo album with pictures of Indian
    and Pakistani celebrations
❖ Mendhi and pattern book
❖ jewellery
❖ mirrors
❖ chalk for Rangoli patterns
❖ picture and story books (dual language if possible)
❖ Indian clothes (male and female) including
    sari lengths
❖ Indian cooking utensils
❖ recipes for chappatis and bhajis
❖ ingredients for cooking
❖ photos of Indian and Pakistani food
❖ tape of Indian music
❖ examples of writing in Indian and Pakistani
    languages
❖ fairy lights to decorate the play area for Diwali
❖ ornaments, pictures, postcards

Suggested activities

- ❖ cooking sweets, chapatis, bhajis, jewel rice.
- ❖ taste different foods.
- ❖ make invitations to a Diwali party.
- ❖ invite parents, children from other schools to share Diwali; learn about Indian dance, putting on a sari.
- ❖ explore Bhangra dancing.
- ❖ listen to Indian music.
- ❖ make clay divas (Diwali lamps) from clay or salt dough.
- ❖ make Rangoli and Mendhi patterns.
- ❖ visit a local temple.
- ❖ visit an Asian grocer's shop.

Rhymes & stories

- ❖ Diwali is Coming
- ❖ Indian music
- ❖ Rama and Sita
- ❖ Let's go to the Temple
- ❖ I am a Hindu
- ❖ Poems about Festivals (Andrew Fusek Peters)

Curriculum links

- ❖ PSD: awareness of needs and views of self & others; respect for own & others' views, cultures, beliefs
- ❖ LCL: vocabulary, different languages
- ❖ K/u: own & others' cultures & beliefs
- ❖ Cr: imagination in music, dance, role play

Title and focus of prop box
'Busy Scissors - at the Hairdresser's'
Focus - hairdressing

Contents of prop box

- ❖ old hairdriers
- ❖ combs and brushes (clean & disinfected)
- ❖ chair
- ❖ towels
- ❖ mirror
- ❖ posters
- ❖ style books with male and female styles
- ❖ magazines and newspapers
- ❖ telephone and phone book
- ❖ receptionist desk
- ❖ appointment book and pen
- ❖ appointment cards
- ❖ purses and money, till
- ❖ rollers and clips, wigs (washed)
- ❖ empty shampoo, conditioner and hairspray bottles
- ❖ a sink or bowl for washing
- ❖ a highlighting cap
- ❖ coffee mugs
- ❖ ribbons, bows, clips etc
- ❖ open/closed sign
- ❖ dolls to use as babies
- ❖ capes or waterproof aprons and staff overalls
- ❖ old mobile phones

The Little Book of Prop Boxes for Role Play

Suggested activities

- ❖ a hairdo for a special day.
- ❖ prepare or a wedding.
- ❖ look at hairdressing magazines; choose a new hairstyle.
- ❖ a mobile hairdresser, using one of the bikes and a mobile case of equipment.
- ❖ make wigs with wool and curled paper.
- ❖ take photos of new hair styles.
- ❖ take the baby for a haircut.
- ❖ have a manicure.
- ❖ visit a local hairdresser or invite them to visit you.
- ❖ measure, compare and look at hair.

Rhymes & stories

- ❖ Need a Trim, Jim?*
- ❖ Rapunzel

- ❖ Hairy McLairy

Curriculum links

- ❖ PSD: work as part of a group
- ❖ LCL: interact & negotiate with others; extend vocabulary; use language to imagine & create roles, know that print carries meaning
- ❖ M: money, time, days
- ❖ K/U: own & others' cultures & beliefs
- ❖ Cr: imagination in role play

Title and focus of prop box
'Stars in Their Eyes'
Focus - music and TV

Contents of prop box

❖ old curtain on a string, a box with 'screen' cut out of front, puppet theatre, table on its side for stage or screen
❖ a glittery curtain
❖ microphone
❖ music collection on tape or CD (a good range is important, and make sure they are groups the children know!)
❖ pop photos and posters
❖ mirror
❖ clean brushes and combs
❖ face paint/make-up/hair 'gel'
❖ jewellery
❖ wigs (washed)
❖ stick on tattoos
❖ pop magazines
❖ cameras
❖ old mobile phones
❖ sparkly clothes, bow ties, feather boas
❖ glamour shoes, bags
❖ guitars and other musical instruments
❖ laminated pictures of stars and other famous people for ideas

Suggested activities

- ❖ have a fancy dress hire shop next to the stage.
- ❖ use the clothes for a fashion show.
- ❖ video a pop star or two and talk about how they move and sing.
- ❖ have a concert and invite the parents.
- ❖ make up a song using home made or bought instruments.
- ❖ make tape recordings of the singers.
- ❖ have a band with drums, bells etc as well as guitars.
- ❖ have an award ceremony with medals or trophies.
- ❖ have a karaoke session or a concert.

Rhymes & stories

- ❖ popular songs
- ❖ advertising jingles
- ❖ signature tunes

Curriculum links

- ❖ PSD: work as part of a group
- ❖ LCL: interact & negotiate with others; extend vocabulary; use language to imagine & create roles; organise, sequence ideas & thoughts
- ❖ M: money, time, days
- ❖ Phys: move with imagination
- ❖ Cr: use imagination in music, dance; express feelings

Title and focus of prop box
'Teeth 'R' Us'
Focus - going to the dentist

Contents of prop box

- ❖ toothbrushes
- ❖ toothpaste
- ❖ pen lights or small torches
- ❖ plaster impressions of teeth (ask a dentist)
- ❖ a dentist's chair
- ❖ plastic mirrors
- ❖ posters (try asking the health centre or dentist)
- ❖ magazines, comics and newspapers for waiting room
- ❖ telephone and phone book, computer
- ❖ receptionist desk, till, credit card machine
- ❖ appointment book and pen
- ❖ appointment cards
- ❖ purses and money
- ❖ file folders
- ❖ forms to fill in (draw one then photocopy)
- ❖ overalls or smocks for dentists
- ❖ badges
- ❖ plastic beakers for rinsing, tissues
- ❖ x-ray pictures of teeth
- ❖ clip boards
- ❖ TV or radio for waiting room
- ❖ stickers for brave children or no treatment

Suggested activities

- ❖ emergency appointments and regular check ups.
- ❖ regular checkups.
- ❖ good food for teeth.
- ❖ invite the dentist to visit.
- ❖ terrible toothache - how would you feel?
- ❖ what do dentists do - perhaps a visit to your local dentist.
- ❖ tooth counts.
- ❖ how to brush and look after your teeth.
- ❖ do animals have dentists?

Rhymes & stories

- ❖ Visiting the Dentist*
- ❖ Going to the Dentist*
- ❖ Monster's Terrible Toothache*
- ❖ I'm a Little Toothbrush (from "I'm a Little Teapot")

Curriculum links

- ❖ PSD: work as part of a group
- ❖ LCL: interact & negotiate with others, taking turns in con versation; extend vocabulary; use language to imagine & create roles; writing
- ❖ M: counting, time
- ❖ K/U:find out about environment/things they like/dislike
- ❖ Cr: imagination in role play & stories

Title and focus of prop box
'The Royal Box - Kings and Queens'
Focus - being famous

Contents of prop box

- ❖ crowns and tiaras
- ❖ jewellery
- ❖ rings
- ❖ throne - velvet draped over a chair
- ❖ handbags
- ❖ gold accessories, chains, medals etc
- ❖ gloves
- ❖ elaborate wallpaper to decorate the house
- ❖ pictures in gold frames
- ❖ special teasets
- ❖ candlesticks and candles
- ❖ lace tablecloths and doileys
- ❖ silver trays
- ❖ robes
- ❖ capes and cloaks
- ❖ tights
- ❖ old bridesmaids' and pages' outfits
- ❖ shoes (add foil covered buckles)
- ❖ evening dresses and shoes
- ❖ sailor and soldier caps
- ❖ top hats, garden party hats
- ❖ wigs (make sure they're washed!)
- ❖ cap for chauffeur

Suggested activities

- ❖ have a royal wedding.
- ❖ have a procession.
- ❖ royal visitors to the classroom.
- ❖ collect picture of royal families.
- ❖ make crowns.
- ❖ take photos of your royals for a photo album.
- ❖ have a royal feast or banquet.
- ❖ read or watch Sleeping Beauty.
- ❖ practise walking like a king or queen.
- ❖ use a trike, trolley etc. as a royal car with a driver.
- ❖ make flags, bunting and banners.

Rhymes & stories

- ❖ The Happy Princess*
- ❖ I Want my Potty!*
- ❖ Princess Cinders*
- ❖ The Queen's Knickers*
- ❖ King Rollo*
- ❖ There was a Princess Long Ago
- ❖ Old King Cole

Curriculum links

- ❖ PSD: work as part of a group, maintain attention
- ❖ LCL: interact & negotiate with others; extend vocabulary; use language to imagine & create roles; retell stories in own words
- ❖ K/U: past and present
- ❖ Cr: imagination in role play

Title and focus of prop box
'Washing Day'
Focus - the laundry or laundromat

Contents of prop box

- ❖ aprons
- ❖ a wide range of clothes of different sizes, colours, types including babies' and dolls' clothes
- ❖ towels, tablecloths, teatowels etc
- ❖ socks, gloves etc in pairs
- ❖ washing baskets, washing line
- ❖ soap powders (empty boxes or bottles)
- ❖ conditioners (empty bottles)
- ❖ open/closed notice
- ❖ iron and ironing board
- ❖ clock, till and money, pens and pencils
- ❖ coins or tokens for machines
- ❖ overalls for laundry staff
- ❖ lost property box label
- ❖ magazines and newspapers

Larger equipment
- ❖ chairs for waiting
- ❖ large cardboard boxes with the fronts cut out in a circle for the door, painted white to use as machines (you could have front and top loaders)
- ❖ litter bins
- ❖ drink machine (a narrow box with empty drink cans and a slot for money)

The Little Book of Prop Boxes for Role Play

Suggested activities

❖ sort clothes into colours and types.
❖ pair up a random collection of socks.
❖ put up washing lines indoors or out.
❖ talk about how and why things dry, what happens when things get wet.
❖ retell stories (suggestions below).
❖ discuss different cultures and their clothes.
❖ do real washing outside and hang to dry.
❖ experiment with colours that run - draw on wet paper with felt pens, mix colours in finger paint, tie dye.
❖ folding and sorting clothes.

Rhymes & stories

❖ Mrs Mopple's Washing Line*
❖ Mrs Wishy Washy*
❖ Doing the Washing*
❖ Mrs Lather's Laundry*
❖ The Wind Blew
❖ This is the Way We Wash Our Clothes

Curriculum links

❖ LCL: vocabulary; sequence
❖ M: language such as smaller, heavier; pattern; pairs; money
❖ K/u: Look at similarities, differences, patterns & change; features in the locality
❖ Cr: explore texture in 2 and 3 dimensions; use imagination in role play

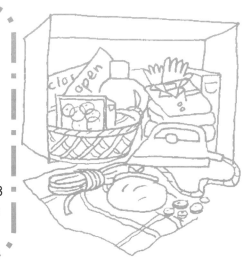

Title and focus of prop box
'The Fast Pizza People'
Focus - Fast food delivery

Contents of prop box

- ❖ pizza boxes (small ones are easier to handle)
- ❖ satchel or carrying bag
- ❖ bike helmet for deliveries
- ❖ menus, including list of toppings (pictorial)
- ❖ money and bag
- ❖ notebook for delivery addresses
- ❖ street map
- ❖ mobile phones
- ❖ telephone
- ❖ telephone directory
- ❖ dough recipes and dough or fake pizzas from salt dough with painted toppings
- ❖ chef's apron, checked trousers, hat
- ❖ pizza wheels
- ❖ paper napkins
- ❖ cutters and rollers
- ❖ magazines and newspapers
- ❖ posters

Larger equipment
- ❖ trike or bike for deliveries
- ❖ large cardboard box with 'door' cut out for oven
- ❖ table for counter
- ❖ chairs to wait on

Suggested activities

- ❖ cook and eat real pizzas, try unfamiliar toppings
- ❖ visit a pizza place
- ❖ talk about making a telephone order - what to say
- ❖ design a pizza combination, real, salt dough or collage
- ❖ look at local street maps and routes to houses, talk about finding your way and getting lost
- ❖ talk about how to keep things warm
- ❖ have an Italian week with food, flags, songs etc
- ❖ order a pizza on the computer!
- ❖ talk about other fast food they know and like, make a graph of favourite foods

Rhymes & stories

- ❖ 'Five Round Pizzas' (as 'Five Currant Buns')

- ❖ 1 hot pizza, 2 hot pizzas, etc. (as in 1 potato, 2 potatoes)

Curriculum links

- ❖ PSD: select and use resources
- ❖ LCL: vocabulary; sequence
- ❖ M: money, counting, number, position & direction
- ❖ K/u: uses of technology; features in the locality, pattern, food and cooking; routes
- ❖ Phys: handle tools, healthy eating
- ❖ Cr: explore texture in 2 and 3 dimensions; use imagination in role play; design and make

Title and focus of prop box
'The Hungry Giants'
Focus - large scale living

Contents of prop box

- ❖ very large salad bowls or mixing bowls
- ❖ large spoons, forks, knives (make from cardboard and cover with foil or silver paint)
- ❖ large cereal packet (make from cardboard box)
- ❖ dry pasta to fill the cereal packet
- ❖ very large plates (cardboard, papier mache or plastic)
- ❖ big table napkins
- ❖ big teapot, cups and saucers
- ❖ big slippers (more than one pair)
- ❖ large adult size clothes (male and female) - tee shirts, trousers, long skirts or dresses, belts
- ❖ big aprons
- ❖ giant's beard, giant glasses
- ❖ big hats
- ❖ big place mats, a big vase of flowers
- ❖ a huge newspaper

Larger equipment
- ❖ big table and chair or bar stool (adult size)
- ❖ large cardboard boxes with the fronts cut out to make a big cupboard
- ❖ a big mirror

Suggested activities

- ❖ make big cups, saucers, plates etc with papier mache or card from boxes
- ❖ setting the table for different meals and numbers
- ❖ use a shoe box to make a home for someone very small
- ❖ make a trail of giant's footprints
- ❖ move like a giant, speak like a giant, act out stories
- ❖ use the computer to enlarge and reduce pictures
- ❖ make a picnic for a giant
- ❖ grow or make some very big flowers for the giants' table

Rhymes & stories

- ❖ The Hungry Giant's Soup*
- ❖ Jack and the Beanstalk
- ❖ Jim and the Beanstalk*
- ❖ The Selfish Giant*
- ❖ This is the Way the Giant Eats (Mulberry Bush tune)
- ❖ Mrs Pepperpot*

Curriculum links

- ❖ LCL: vocabulary of size, sequence in stories, explore sounds and words
- ❖ M: language such as bigger, smaller, heavier
- ❖ K/u: Look at similarities and differences
- ❖ Phys: healthy eating
- ❖ Cr: use imagination in role play and stories

Title and focus of prop box
'Flashing Fire Engines'
Focus - the fire services

Contents of prop box

- ❖ firemen's uniforms
- ❖ helmets, boots
- ❖ gloves
- ❖ phones - mobile and fixed - walkie talkies
- ❖ garden hose
- ❖ Fire Station labels
- ❖ No Parking signs
- ❖ torches, flashlights
- ❖ first aid kit
- ❖ fire safety posters
- ❖ street maps
- ❖ cones
- ❖ flashing lights
- ❖ tape of fire sirens and other sound effects
- ❖ clipboards
- ❖ badges
- ❖ stripey tape to cordon off areas

Larger equipment
- ❖ truck or bikes for fire engines
- ❖ 'pop up' fire engine
- ❖ small step ladder
- ❖ chairs and table for inside fire station
- ❖ tape recorder

Suggested activities

- ❖ fire drills and other emergencies in your setting
- ❖ fire safety, fire officer visit
- ❖ using maps to find your way
- ❖ uniforms and others who help us
- ❖ discuss how you feel and what to do when you are e.g. lost, in danger, locked out
- ❖ Bonfire Night
- ❖ water play with hoses, pumps and pipes
- ❖ using sprays for painting, paint with water outside
- ❖ explore waterproofing and waterproof materials
- ❖ emergency phone numbers, addresses

Rhymes & stories

- ❖ Flashing Fire Engines*
- ❖ Fireman Piggy Wiggy*

- ❖ Fireman Sam books and videos*
- ❖ London's Burning

Curriculum links

- ❖ LCL: use talk, retell narratives, speak clearly, attempt writing, express feelings
- ❖ M: number names
- ❖ K/u: Find out about past and present events; uses of technology
- ❖ Phys: move with control & co-ordination
- ❖ Cr: use imagination in role play

Title and focus of prop box
'For Sale'
Focus - extending domestic role play

Contents of prop box

- ❖ collapsed cardboard boxes (to be re-taped for packing)
- ❖ paper, bubble wrap, newspaper for packing
- ❖ tape, labels
- ❖ toys and crockery to pack up
- ❖ maps
- ❖ 'For Sale', 'For Rent', 'Sold' signs and notices
- ❖ telephone, mobile phone, phone book
- ❖ leaflets from estate agents, newspaper supplements, photo book of different sorts of houses
- ❖ rollers and brushes for 'redecorating'
- ❖ wallpaper, wallpaper books, paint sample cards
- ❖ curtains, nets, blinds
- ❖ paint tins and paint buckets
- ❖ mops and cleaning materials
- ❖ dustpans and brushes
- ❖ keys and locks
- ❖ forms, letters, envelopes
- ❖ gloves and overalls for decorating
- ❖ overalls for removal men
- ❖ kettle, teapot and cups

Larger equipment
- ❖ truck or cart for moving van

Suggested activities

- ❖ pack up the home corner for moving day; move the house from indoors to outdoors, with a new location outside; clean the house; put up signs.
- ❖ have a welcoming party or picnic.
- ❖ talk about moving, choosing a new home, addresses (flats, bungalows, caravans, semi-detached etc.); collect and use estate agents materials, newspaper adverts to discuss different homes and features.
- ❖ do a real 'make over' of the house area, choose new paint and wallpaper, curtains, etc.
- ❖ go for a walk and take photos of different homes.

Rhymes & stories

- ❖ Three Little Pigs
- ❖ Goodbye House*
- ❖ Moving House (3 titles)*
- ❖ Moving Molly*
- ❖ This is Our House*
- ❖ Teddy Bears' Moving Day*

Curriculum links

- ❖ PSD: respond to significant experiences; explore needs and feelings
- ❖ LCL: vocabulary; explore feel ings; recreate experiences
- ❖ M: house numbers, direction and position
- ❖ K/u: Old and new; patterns & change; features in the area
- ❖ Cr: explore texture & colour in 2 and 3 dimensions

The Little Book of Prop Boxes for Role Play

Title and focus of prop box
'Can We Build It?'
Focus - a building site

Contents of prop box

- ❖ buckets and spades
- ❖ plastic or small size tools
- ❖ cones and tape
- ❖ hard hats
- ❖ jeans, checked shirts, fluorescent waistcoats or jackets
- ❖ photos or pictures of different houses
- ❖ clipboards, pens
- ❖ measuring tapes and rulers
- ❖ "CAUTION", "BUILDING SITE", "HARD HAT AREA" signs
- ❖ teapot and mugs
- ❖ tool kit
- ❖ sorting box with nails and screws
- ❖ sandwich boxes
- ❖ plans, diagrams of houses and other buildings
- ❖ camera (real or home made)
- ❖ first aid kit

Larger equipment

- ❖ wooden blocks, large plastic bricks (or real bricks)
- ❖ workmen's hut or pop up tent
- ❖ plastic pipes, pulleys and ropes
- ❖ large construction kits, e.g. Quadro

Suggested activities

- ❖ visit a building site, take photos.
- ❖ design and make a model of a new house for yourself.
- ❖ look at brick patterns and other building materials.
- ❖ use small world in the sand tray to explore building and excavation.
- ❖ look at brick patterns, do rubbings of different textures and surfaces.
- ❖ tape off part of the outside area and 'dig' a hole or build a house; use the platform of the climbing frame to explore pulleys, ropes and pipes.
- ❖ talk about safety and avoiding accidents.

Rhymes & stories

- ❖ Bob the Builder books and videos*
- ❖ Dig, dig, digging*
- ❖ Miss Brick the Builders' Baby*

Curriculum links

- ❖ LCL: vocabulary; sequences, explore new words
- ❖ M: language of size; pattern; measuring
- ❖ K/u: build and construct with a wide range of materials; select tools & techniques; investigate materials
- ❖ Phys: control & co-ordination
- ❖ Cr: explore texture in 2 and 3 dimensions

Title and focus of prop box
'Rock-a-Bye Baby'
Focus - new babies

Contents of prop box

❖ baby dolls, ideally including twins(anatomically correct and from several cultures)
❖ nappies, baby clothes
❖ blankets, baby shawls
❖ baby sling
❖ name labels for babies' wrists
❖ book of baby names
❖ baby soap, powder, cream, wipes etc
❖ baby food in plastic jars and packets
❖ bottles, baby cups, dummies
❖ congratulation cards
❖ camera, baby photo books
❖ baby books, toys, catalogues and magazines
❖ plastic seed propagator (for premature babies!)
❖ baby scales
❖ uniforms for male and female nurses and doctors
❖ medical kit
❖ posters and leaflets

Larger equipment
❖ pushchairs
❖ cots and prams
❖ truck for ambulance
❖ folding bed for mother to be

The Little Book of Prop Boxes for Role Play

Suggested activities

- ❖ visit a baby clinic or ask the health visitor to visit you.
- ❖ write lists of things babies need (pictorial or 'have a go' writing).
- ❖ invite a new mum or dad and their baby to visit.
- ❖ sing and listen to lullabies.
- ❖ tape babies crying, singing, babbling.
- ❖ talk about babies who are premature or sick.
- ❖ collect names for a name book.
- ❖ do a display of baby photos and guess who is which.
- ❖ talk about 'When I was a baby' and 'Now I am bigger'.
- ❖ sort and discuss baby clothes and equipment.

Rhymes & stories

- ❖ Baby Bill and Little Lill*
- ❖ So Many Babies*
- ❖ The Baby Dances*
- ❖ The Babies' Catalogue*

- ❖ So Much*
- ❖ Boom Baby Boom*
- ❖ The New Baby*
- ❖ The Last Noo-Noo*
- ❖ Ben's Baby*
- ❖ A Baby Just Like Me*

Curriculum links

- ❖ PSD: caring for others; past & present events
- ❖ LCL: vocabulary; sequences, lists, cards, imagine and recreate experiences
- ❖ M: language such as smaller, heavier
- ❖ K/u: Look at similarities, differences, patterns, change
- ❖ Cr: use imagination in role play

Title and focus of prop box
'Bears Night and Day'
Focus - retell a specific story "Peace at Last"

Contents of prop box

- ❖ clock
- ❖ newspapers and glasses for Father Bear
- ❖ paper plane and other toys for Baby Bear
- ❖ hairnet and rollers for Mother Bear
- ❖ porridge and recipe
- ❖ bowls and spoons, cutlery, tablecloth
- ❖ toothpaste and brushes
- ❖ toiletries for bedtime
- ❖ pyjamas and nightie
- ❖ sound tape of the sounds from the story
- ❖ breakfast foods (salt dough, plastic or other replicas)
- ❖ place mats, table napkins
- ❖ blackout curtains
- ❖ torches and lanterns
- ❖ toy owl

Larger equipment
- ❖ kitchen furniture
- ❖ window scene (e.g. two pictures, easily changed by the children from day to night)
- ❖ bike, car or truck for Daddy Bear's car
- ❖ tree shape on pole set in concrete block

(This idea can be adapted to support other stories; e.g. The 3 Bears, The Picnic, Cinderella, etc.)

The Little Book of Prop Boxes for Role Play

Suggested activities

❖ replay the story in the play area.
❖ tell and act other stories in the Large Family series.
❖ make a set of sequencing pictures of the day, from getting up to going to bed.
❖ make a tape of sounds linked with times of the day.
❖ collect, handle, wear, use and talk about items to do with bedtime and getting up.
❖ talk about hygiene - teeth cleaning, washing, etc.
❖ make porridge, toast.
❖ talk about the dark; animals and birds of the night.
❖ write lists, labels, reminders.

Rhymes & stories

❖ Peace at Last*
❖ The Three Bears*
❖ Owl Babies*
❖ Monster Can't Sleep*

❖ Moonlight*
❖ Sunshine*
❖ A Dark, Dark Tale
❖ Burglar Bill*

Curriculum links

❖ LCL: vocabulary; sequencing events and stories; text on packages and lists
❖ M: time, number, counting
❖ K/u: features of events they experience; events in their own lives; ICT (tapes)
❖ Phys: keeping healthy
❖ Cr: use imagination; respond to what they see and hear; sound recognition

Title and focus of prop box
'Shining Wheels'
Focus - Car wash (outdoors)

Contents of prop box

- ❖ buckets, sponges
- ❖ cloths
- ❖ brushes (various)
- ❖ 'Car Wash', 'Entry', 'Exit' signs
- ❖ cones, chalk for car parking lines, arrows etc.
- ❖ price list
- ❖ car shampoos, etc. (empty bottles)
- ❖ open/closed notice
- ❖ old garden hose
- ❖ clock, till and money, computer keyboard, appointments book, pens and pencils
- ❖ watering cans
- ❖ caps, boots, overalls for car washers
- ❖ lost property box label
- ❖ magazines and newspapers

Larger equipment
- ❖ trikes, cars etc for washing
- ❖ use a large cardboard box to make a tunnel for the car wash. Cut holes in the sides and use long handled brushes to wash the car inside.
- ❖ ...or use a play tunnel

(Another version of this activity uses a piece of drainpipe and toy cars)

Suggested activities

❖ visit a car wash and watch what happens.
❖ talk about how car washes work, what you say, what the washers do.
❖ make a car wash token machine from a box, talk about the difference between tokens and real money.
❖ explore the difference soap or detergent makes to cleaning things.
❖ talk about what happens when things get wet, and how and why things dry; look at puddles drying.
❖ draw car tracks and directions on the ground.
❖ blow bubbles and talk about the colours.

Rhymes & stories

❖ The Car Wash
(recording by Rose Royce)
❖ This is the Way We Wash the Cars/Bikes

❖ Doing the Washing*
❖ Mr Gumpy's Car*

Curriculum links

❖ LCL: interact with others, negotiating activities
❖ M: money; counting
❖ K/u: technology in everyday life; observe and find out about features in everyday life; use tools
❖ Phys: use small and large equipment; handling tools
❖ Cr: use imagination in role play

Title and focus of prop box
'Happy Birthday to You!'
Focus - birthday parties

Contents of prop box

- ❖ paper party plates or plastic picnic sets
- ❖ paper cups, straws, empty plastic drink bottles
- ❖ plastic cutlery
- ❖ balloons, streamers
- ❖ table napkins, tablecloths
- ❖ cards, wrapping paper, gift tags, ribbon
- ❖ boxes and tins to wrap for presents
- ❖ telephone, message pad and pen
- ❖ address book, invitations
- ❖ badges with ages on
- ❖ tape cassette of party games, music and songs
- ❖ recipe book with party food and 'ingredients'
- ❖ salt dough or plastic party food - cakes, sand wiches, pizzas, crisps etc
- ❖ Birthday cake made from a round box or tin, decorated with plaster or paint icing and decorations, candles on top
- ❖ party clothes for boys and girls
- ❖ clothes for an entertainer (magician's cape and hat, clown suit etc)

<u>Larger equipment</u>
- ❖ table and chairs (try garden furniture for a change), cupboard

The Little Book of Prop Boxes for Role Play

Suggested activities

- ❖ make a birthday cake, discuss ingredients, sequence, change.
- ❖ setting the table.
- ❖ practice and discuss the sequence of games, taking turns, following rules.
- ❖ make a photo book of a real party, including preparation, organising, clearing up.
- ❖ find out about deliveries - cards, presents, flowers.
- ❖ parties in different places - picnics, McDonalds, etc.
- ❖ make cards, print wrapping paper.
- ❖ have a magic show or puppets for entertainment.

Rhymes & stories

- ❖ Happy Birthday song
- ❖ action songs and rhymes
- ❖ party games

- ❖ The Birthday Party
- ❖ Titch
- ❖ Sleeping Beauty

Curriculum links

- ❖ PSD: share and take turns
- ❖ LCL: use language to recall and retell experiences; purposes of writing
- ❖ M: explore shape, size, bigger, smaller; pattern; number
- ❖ K/u: explore change; past & present events
- ❖ Cr: use imagination in role play

Title and focus of prop box
'Gone Fishing' (good for outside)
Focus - hobbies and interests

Contents of prop box

- ❖ fishing nets, fishing rods with floats (telescopic ones are fascinating to children)
- ❖ folding chairs or stools
- ❖ umbrellas or sunshades
- ❖ blue fabric or plastic sheeting for a river or pond
- ❖ plants in pots for edge of river
- ❖ plastic insects to hang on strings or float on the 'water'
- ❖ frogs, toads, newts (plastic)
- ❖ plastic fish (or use some from a magnetic fishing game, and put magnets on the ends of the fishing lines
- ❖ keep net or plastic box for things caught
- ❖ reference and identification books about river life and fish
- ❖ background tape with country and watery sounds
- ❖ green netting with leaves and twigs to make a screen for the area
- ❖ bush hats, green anoraks, body warmers, waterproofs, wellies

Larger equipment
- ❖ deck chairs
- ❖ big umbrellas

The Little Book of Prop Boxes for Role Play

Suggested activities

- ❖ fill the water tray with water and plastic fish; use small dipping nets to catch and count fish.
- ❖ visit the fishmongers or a supermarket to look at (and buy) some fish; smell, touch & cook them to eat.
- ❖ as an alternative to a harvest festival, try a "Harvest from the Sea" celebration.
- ❖ make a boat from a big box or construction sets. Go fishing with nets over the side.
- ❖ watch a video or a TV programme of fishermen.
- ❖ talk about waterproofing.
- ❖ make an aquarium with real or pretend fish.

Rhymes & stories

- ❖ Row, Row, Row the Boat
- ❖ 1, 2, 3, 4, 5
- ❖ Mr Gumpy's Outing*
- ❖ The Little Boat*
- ❖ Noah's Ark
- ❖ Sally and the Limpet*

Curriculum links

- ❖ PSD: maintain attention & sit
- ❖ LCL: vocabulary; recounting experiences
- ❖ M: number; shape, size
- ❖ K/u: find out about living things; look closely
- ❖ Phys: use a range of equipment
- ❖ Cr: explore colour, texture, shape; use imagination in role play

Title and focus of prop box
'Fast Food to Go!'
Focus – sandwich bar or organic cafe

Contents of prop box

- ❖ small blackboard and chalk
- ❖ lunch boxes, bags
- ❖ sandwiches (real or made from thin sponge and paint)
- ❖ aprons, overalls, plastic gloves, caps or hairnets
- ❖ cutlery, spreaders, blunt knives
- ❖ chopping boards
- ❖ containers for food
- ❖ open/closed notice
- ❖ till and money
- ❖ telephone and message pad
- ❖ posters, lists of sandwich fillings, prices
- ❖ badges for staff
- ❖ empty flasks and drink bottles
- ❖ laminated pictures and photos of food
- ❖ food covers
- ❖ teatowel, washing up bowl

Larger equipment
- ❖ chairs for waiting
- ❖ table for eating in
- ❖ litter bin
- ❖ drink machine (a narrow box with empty drink cans and a slot for money)

Suggested activities

❖ collect some ingredients, make up a new sandwich filling and taste it.
❖ record the sequence of sandwich making in photos.
❖ discuss and record likes and dislikes in sandwiches.
❖ explore different sorts of bread, visit a baker.
❖ use cutters to try different shapes for sandwiches.
❖ make bags for sandwiches (paper) and decorate.
❖ talk about and design some logos.
❖ make menus with pictures or 'have a go' writing.
❖ try different tools for cutting and spreading.
❖ make spiral sandwiches by rolling up the bread.

Rhymes & stories

❖ The Giant Jam Sandwich*
❖ This is the Way We Make a Sandwich
❖ Bread and Jam*
❖ Pass the Jam Jim

Curriculum links

❖ PSD: personal hygiene
❖ LCL: writing lists; food vocabulary; sequencing
❖ M: vocabulary of shape & size
❖ K/u: talk about likes & dislikes
❖ Phys: handle tools safely; understand the importance of healthy eating
❖ Cr: respond to what they see, smell, touch & feel

Title and focus of prop box
'Our Body Shop'
Focus - body care

Contents of prop box

- ❖ empty plastic bottles, labelled and filled with coloured water, price tags, sticky labels
- ❖ old perfume bottles and sprays (empty)
- ❖ collection of soaps
- ❖ food flavourings and essences to create smells (banana, strawberry, peppermint)
- ❖ herbs and other natural scents (mint, lavender)
- ❖ shelves and surfaces for display
- ❖ small bowls and tine spoons to make 'potions' and perfumes
- ❖ small empty plastic bottles
- ❖ small wooden sticks to try the perfumes
- ❖ clock, till and money, pens and pencils
- ❖ posters of flowers, herbs, cosmetics
- ❖ overalls/uniforms and badges for staff
- ❖ leaflets from chemists
- ❖ mirrors

Larger equipment
- ❖ chairs for waiting
- ❖ a table for testing the products

NB. Check for allergies among the children. It's always safest to use coloured water and natural flavourings and colourings.

Suggested activities

❖ talk about perfumes and body care.
❖ try some aromatherapy oils (adult supervision essential).
❖ mix things, making rose water or Tea Tree 'perfume'.
❖ use empty bottles in the water tray to fill & empty.
❖ make price lists, bottle labels, price tags.
❖ talk about nice and nasty smells, preferences, dislikes.
❖ use flower petals, lavender and other herbs to make perfume bags with squares of net and ribbon (a good gift for Mothers' Day).
❖ collect and press flowers and leaves to make pictures, labels and to decorate bags for the shop.

Rhymes & stories

❖ The Smelly Book*
❖ Nice and Nasty*
❖ 5 bottles of Bubble Bath in the Body Care Shop
❖ 5 Shampoo Bottles
❖ This is the Way we Wash our Hair (Put on Lotion, etc.)

Curriculum links

❖ PSD: select and use resources independently
❖ LCL: use talk to organise
❖ M: vocabulary of capacity
❖ K/u: talk about likes & dislikes; use senses to explore; find out about plants
❖ Phys: handle tools safely; pour, fill empty, transfer
❖ Cr: respond to what they see, smell, touch & feel

Title and focus of prop box
'Come and Read'
Focus - a library

Contents of prop box

- ❖ inkpads and stamps
- ❖ a wide range of books for children
- ❖ adult paperbacks
- ❖ magazines and newspapers
- ❖ library cards (laminated to make them look shiny)
- ❖ notices, forms
- ❖ book posters, book covers, catalogues (ask your local bookshop or write to publishers)
- ❖ open/closed notice
- ❖ computer (real or home made)
- ❖ scanner to scan bar codes
- ❖ badges for librarians, glasses
- ❖ telephone and message pad
- ❖ writing materials
- ❖ adult and children's clothes for visitors to library
- ❖ bags for books

Larger equipment
- ❖ comfortable chairs, bean bags, cushions
- ❖ shelves and stands for books
- ❖ table for librarian
- ❖ trolley for books
- ❖ pushchair and doll

The Little Book of Prop Boxes for Role Play

Suggested activities

❖ visit your local library or ask a librarian to visit you.
❖ have a repair session and let the children help with mending books, to promote care.
❖ make zig-zag and big books for the library.
❖ make photo books.
❖ act out favourite stories.
❖ encourage children to read to each other or even to a group.
❖ talk about the different sorts of books (fiction, non fiction) and about the different sections in a library.
❖ match the real book to a photocopy of the cover.

Rhymes & stories

❖ Before you read a book, look at the cover, the author, the illustrator. Talk about favourite stories and those from favourite authors or illustrators. Show children how to turn pages and return books to shelves carefully.

Curriculum links

❖ LCL: recalling stories; enjoyment of stories
❖ M: counting; size; sorting
❖ K/u: Look at features in the locality; sources of information
❖ Phys: move with control and co-ordination
❖ Cr: looking carefully at pictures in books; use imagination in role play

Title and focus of prop box
'Very Interesting!'
Focus - museums

Contents of prop box

- ❖ famous paintings mounted and framed with gold paper or braid
- ❖ plastic minibeasts in small boxes (plastic or card)
- ❖ collect bric a brac from rummage sales and car boots. Ask parents if they have interesting things to lend or donate
- ❖ signs and labels (THIS WAY, WAY IN, EXIT, TOILETS, SHOP, TICKETS etc)
- ❖ thick cord for making a route or queue (fix on stands (see below)
- ❖ posters (the children can draw or paint these)
- ❖ leaflets, booklets etc
- ❖ tickets
- ❖ till and money, pens and pencils
- ❖ reference books
- ❖ uniforms and badges for staff

Larger equipment
- ❖ make stands for notices by filling a bucket with sand or cement and sticking a broom handle in it

NB. Your museum could be for natural history, painting, science or antiquities. You could also have a display of children's paintings, celebrate local cultures, local history, photography etc

Suggested activities

❖ visit a museum to get ideas for your own.
❖ look at and discuss unfamiliar objects and what they might be.
❖ make 3D models and put them in an art gallery; invite parents to come.
❖ make a dinosaur collection.
❖ make labels and notices.
❖ talk about security and valuables; make a CCTV camera.
❖ take photos of the things in the collection and make a catalogue.
❖ have a museum shop with postcards and gifts.

Rhymes & stories

❖ Talk about the different sorts of literature- books, magazines, leaflets, catalogues, fic- tion and non-fiction books. Discuss what is old and what is new; how people find old things and then find out what they are.

Curriculum links

❖ PSD: develop respect for own and other cultures
❖ LCL: ask questions about where, why, who
❖ M: time
❖ K/u: find out about past and present events and objects; features of the place where they live
❖ Cr: respond to what they see, smell, touch & feel

Title and focus of prop box
'In a Jungle'
Focus - a rain forest

Contents of prop box

❖ bead or bamboo curtains
❖ bean netting, green material or camouflage net
❖ tape recording of rain forest sounds
❖ cut out pictures of rain forest animals and birds
   to hang from ceiling (laminating with make them
   more durable)
❖ wind chimes
❖ binoculars
❖ sleeping bags, shorts, boots, hats
❖ compass, rucksack, water bottles
❖ sketch pads and pencils, notebooks
❖ cameras
❖ torches and battery lanterns
❖ wood for a pretend fire
❖ picnic set
❖ wind chimes

Larger equipment
❖ pop up tent
❖ wheeled toy for explorers' jeep

This is a good activity for outside. Hang netting from a fixed climbing frame and camp underneath.
Or you could make a day and night indoor rain forest.

Suggested activities

- ❖ talk about making dens and camps.
- ❖ cook camping food (real or pretend).
- ❖ listen to the forest sounds and depict them in painting or drawing.
- ❖ move like animals, follow tracks.
- ❖ look at exotic plants and animals (real, in books or on video).
- ❖ talk about being brave and scared and being out at night or in a strange place.
- ❖ make animal masks.
- ❖ make jungle music.

Rhymes & stories

- ❖ The Rainforest*
- ❖ Pirates Ahoy*
- ❖ We're going on a Bear Hunt*
- ❖ jungle music
- ❖ 5 Fierce Tigers in a Big Forest

Curriculum links

- ❖ PSD: work in a group; respond to experiences, express feelings
- ❖ LCL: use talk to organise & recreate experiences
- ❖ K/u: use senses to explore; find out about plants & animals; discuss likes & dislikes
- ❖ Cr: respond to what they see, smell, touch & feel

Title and focus of prop box
'Let's Go!'
Focus - travel agent

Contents of prop box

- ❖ travel brochures and leaflets, posters & photos
- ❖ computer
- ❖ forms to fill in
- ❖ maps, atlases and globes
- ❖ tickets (draw some, then photocopy)
- ❖ till, money
- ❖ travellers' cheques, foreign money to exchange
- ❖ suitcases, hand luggage packed with holiday clothes
- ❖ cameras, sunhats, binoculars
- ❖ goggles, flippers, arm bands
- ❖ labels for bags
- ❖ photo books with pictures of hotels, swimming pools etc
- ❖ overalls/uniforms and badges for staff

Larger equipment
- ❖ chairs for waiting
- ❖ table for travel agents

NB. If you really want to expand this theme, have an aeroplane or a coach to take people to the holiday places. Then you need uniforms, pilots' or coach drivers' cases and caps, trolleys for in-travel catering. Find out how and where most of your children go on holiday and build on these experiences first before introducing more exotic destinations!

The Little Book of Prop Boxes for Role Play

Suggested activities

- ❖ talk about holidays and where your children go.
- ❖ make tickets and posters.
- ❖ paint pictures of holidays,
- ❖ ask parents to send in photos, make a photo album.
- ❖ ask children to send postcards to the class when they go away.
- ❖ share stories about journeys and discuss excitement and fears.
- ❖ write to travel firms to get information and posters.
- ❖ visit a travel agent; watch a travel programme.
- ❖ look at maps, globes and atlases, talk about weather.

Rhymes & stories

- ❖ Sally and the Limpet*
- ❖ We're all Going on a Summer Holiday
- ❖ Alfie Outdoors*
- ❖ The Wheels on the Bus (Doors on the Train, propellors on the boat

Curriculum links

- ❖ PSD: discuss feelings
- ❖ LCL: use talk to organise & sequence; purposes of writing; use language to imagine & recreate experiences
- ❖ M: time, distance, day & night; money
- ❖ K/u: find out about events
- ❖ Cr: respond to what they see, smell, touch & feel; use imagination in role play

Dear Parent/Carer

We are developing the role play resources in our setting to help your child understand many different aspects of learning. The new boxes will also help all the children to develop their vocabulary and social skills. When we have collected items we intend to sort and store them carefully in collections linked to different sorts of play. These will be our new 'Prop Boxes', and we hope you will see them in use very soon.

We are asking for your help in making the prop boxes interesting and varied. Can you have a look at home or on your travels for the following items?

....

....

....

....

....

Please bring these to us as you find them.

Thank you for your help.

Yours sincerely

Title of prop box:

Contents list:
Clothes

Other items

Additional resources needed

Evaluation notes

Disposable items needing replacement

Book List

Title	Author
The Lighthouse Keeper's Lunch	Ronda & David Armitage
Hello Beaky	Jez Alborough
Lance's Lunchtime	
I am Hindu, I am a Sikh	
Need a Trim, Jim?	Kaye Umanski
Everybody's Hair	Joan Solomon
Visiting the Dentist	Althea
Going to the Dentist	A Civardi
Monster's Terrible Toothache	Impey Rose
The Paper Bag Princess	Robert N Mursch
The Happy Princess	Nicholas Allan
Princess Cinders	Babbette Cole
The Queen's Knickers	Nicholas Allen
Pointy Hatted Princesses	Nick Sharratt
King Rollo's Autumn	David Mckee
Jamelas Dress (weddings)	Nicki Daly
Doing the Washing	Sarah Garland
Mrs Wishy Washy	Big Book
Mrs Lather's Laundry	Allan Ahlberg
Baby Loves Hugs and Kisses	Michael Lawrence
Mrs Moppple's Washing Line	
The Wind Blew	Pat Hutchins
All Fall Down	Helen Oxenbury
Pete's a Pizza	William Steig
The Hungry Giant's Soup	Joy Cowley (big book)
The Selfish Giant	Oscar Wilde
Jim and the Beanstalk	Raymond Briggs
Flashing Fire Engines	Tony Mitten
Fireman Piggy Wiggy	Diane Fax
Fireman Sam books and videos	

The Little Book of Prop Boxes for Role Play

Title	Author
Goodbye House	F Asch
Moving House	A Civardi
Moving Molly	Shirley Hughes
Moving House	C Jessel
Moving House	K Petty
This is My House	M Rosen
Helpers	Shirley Hughes
Keeping House	Margaret Mahy
Dig, Dig, Digging	Margaret Mayo
Miss Brick the Builder's Daughter	Allan Ahlberg
Baby Bill and Little Lil	Sue Heap
So Many Babies	Martina Selway
Boom Baby Boom	Margaret Mahy
So Much	Trish Cooke
Ben's Baby	Michael Foreman
The Last Noo-Noo	Jill Murphy
The Babies' Catalogue	Janet & Allan Ahlberg
The Baby Dances	Kathy Henderson
A Baby Just Like Me	Susan Winter
Pet's Little Princess	Tony Ross
Peace at Last	Jill Murphy
It's The Bear	Jez Alborough
Monster Can't Sleep	Virginia Mueller
When the Teddy Bears Came	Martin Waddell
Moonlight & Sunshine	Jan Ormerod
Burglar Bill	Allan Ahlberg
Mr Gumpy's Car	John Burningham
Having a Picnic	Sarah Garland
Coming to Tea	Sarah Garland
Mr Gumpy's Outing	John Burningham
The Little Boat	Kathy Henderson
Sally and the Limpet	Simon James

Title	Author
The Giant Jam Sandwich	
Pass the Jam Jim	Kaye Umanski
The Smelly Book	
Nice and Nasty	Nick Butterworth
Forest Singer	Sylvia Sikundar
Rainforest	Helen Cowcher
Pirates Ahoy	Hilary McKay
Alfie Outdoors	Shirley Hughes
Doing the Gardening	Sarah Garland
Going Shopping	Sarah Garland
Katie Morag and the Wedding	Marie Hedderwick
Poems about festivals	Andre Fusek Peters
This Little Puffin	Penguin Books

The Little Book of Prop Boxes for Role Play

Did you enjoy this Little Book?
Would you like to see more?

Then join
The Little Books Club!

- Members get <u>each new title as soon as it is published</u>
- <u>Special discount prices</u>
- All books sent <u>on approval</u>
- You don't have to accept any book if you don't want it, and there is <u>no minimum number of books you must take</u>

Interested?

1. Tear out or copy this form.
2. <u>Fill in your details on the other side</u>.
3. Send it to the address given overleaf. (NB. no stamp needed)

Little Books Club Enrolment Form

Name (Mr/Mrs/Miss/Ms) _____

Department/Position (if applicable) _____

School/setting/organisation _____

Address _____

Post Code _____ Phone _____ E-mail _____

Please enrol me in the Little Books Club and send me all future Little Books on 14 days approval as soon as they are published. I have signed and dated this application, and (where applicable) included my credit/debit card details for future payments. I understand that you will not charge my card for any books until I have accepted them. I am under no obligation to accept any book, and may cancel this instruction at any time.

Signed _____ Date _____

(Sorry - we are unable to accept an application without a signature)

Method of payment

☐ Send an invoice with each book and I will pay by cheque (schools, nurseries & similar approved organisations only)

☐ I authorise you to charge for the cost of each book to my Visa/Master Card/Delta/Switch card no:

Issue no. (Switch) _____   Expiry date _____

☎ phone: 0185 888 1212   🖷 fax: 0185 888 1360

💻 e-mail: post:
sales@featherstone.uk.com   Featherstone Education
                                FREEPOST MID 18874
                                Lutterworth LE17 4BR

NB. This FREEPOST address is available for <u>Little Books Club</u> <u>applications and payments only</u>.